What's in this book

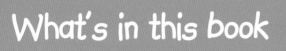

This book belongs to

_____

献爱心 A helping hand

学习内容 Contents

沟通 Communication

问问某人是谁
Ask who or whom someone is

询问及回答谁是物品主人
Ask and respond to questions about personal belongings

生词 New words

★	是	to be
★	谁	who, whom
★	这	this
★	那	that
★	男孩	boy
★	女孩	girl
	铅笔	pencil
	本子	notebook
	足球	football

他是谁?
Who is he?

这是谁的铅笔?
Whose pencil is this?

那是不是你的铅笔?
Is that your pencil?

那是/不是我的铅笔。
That is/is not my pencil.

跨学科学习 Project

将物品分类以便回收,利用
废纸制作手工
Sort items for recycling and
make crafts from scrap paper

文化 Cultures

中国古代足球
Ancient Chinese football

Get ready

1 What is the poster about?

2 Do you have similar posters in your school?

3 What would you do?

他是谁？ 这是谁的铅笔？
谁的本子？

这是我的。

那是他的。

他是……这是我的铅笔。
那是他的本子。

那是谁的足球?

那是男孩的足球。那是我们的！

nǚ hái
女孩

那是女孩的足球。那不是我们的！

我们的东西，能帮助他
人吗？

Let's think

1 What did the children donate? Tick the boxes and write the
correct letters in the blanks.

这是我的 _a_ 。

这是我们的 ____ 。

这是我的 ____ 。

这是我的 ____ 。

2 How can these items help the children
in need? Discuss with your friend.

New words

1 Learn the new words.

女孩

本子

足球

铅笔

男孩

谁

这 是

那

2 Complete the sentences. Write the letters.

a 这　b 那　c 女孩　d 男孩　e 不　f 谁

1

___是 ___
的足球。

2

___是 ___
的足球吗？

3

这是___
的本子？

4

这 ___是
我的铅笔。

11

 1 Listen and circle the correct pictures.

1

2

3

ory and say.

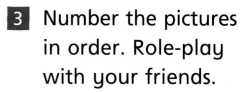

这是我的铅笔。

这是谁的铅笔？

是不是爸爸的？

那不是我的铅笔。

Task

Role-play with your friends. Find the owners of the lost items.

Song

 05 Listen and sing.

这是谁的铅笔？

那是谁的本子？

铅笔是我的，

本子是他的。

铅笔不是他的，

本子不是你的，

这是我的，你的呢？

课堂用语 Classroom language

别叫。
Don't shout.

别说话。
Don't talk.

15

1 Trace the strokes to complete the characters.

日 目 妈

眼 鱼 早

2 Learn the component. Circle 田 in the characters.

田 鱼 男 画 由

3 How many 田 can you find? Circle the correct answer.

a 十三

a 九

c 十

d 五

4 Trace and write the character.

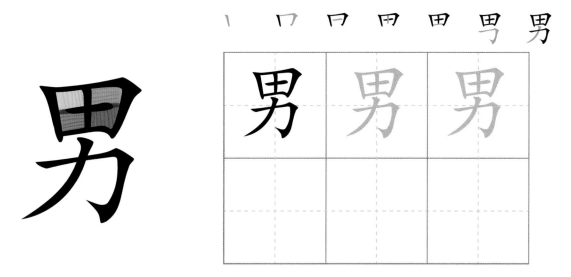

男 男 男 男

汉字小常识 Did you know?

> Two or more components combined can give a clue to the meaning of a character.

田 (field) and 力 (strength) combined mean 'man'/'men'. This is because in ancient China, men worked in the fields.

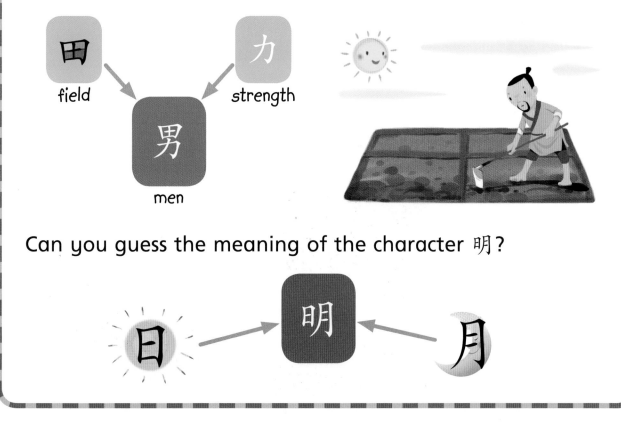

Can you guess the meaning of the character 明?

Cultures

1 Learn about ancient Chinese football.

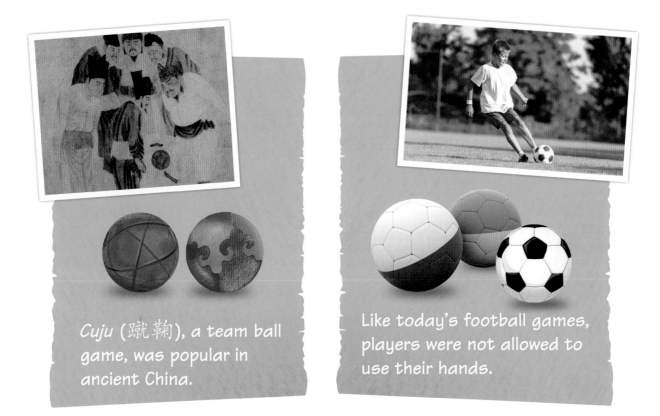

Cuju (蹴鞠), a team ball game, was popular in ancient China.

Like today's football games, players were not allowed to use their hands.

2 Circle the Chinese football in the old paintings.

1 Where should the items go? Match them to the right places.

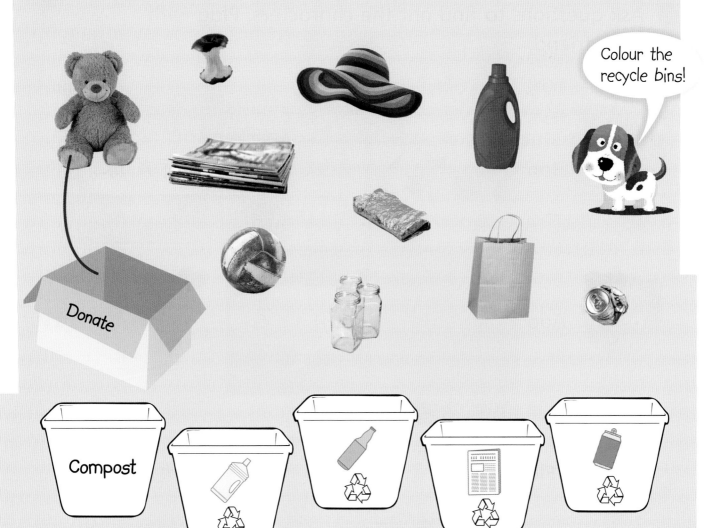

Colour the recycle bins!

Donate

Compost

2 Do not throw away used paper, make art!

① ② ③

温习 Checkpoint

1 Ask questions to find out the characters. Play with your friend.

2 Work with your friend. Colour the stars and the chillies.

Words			
是	☆	☆	🌶
谁	☆	☆	🌶
这	☆	☆	🌶
那	☆	☆	🌶
男孩	☆	☆	🌶
女孩	☆	☆	🌶
铅笔	☆	🌶	🌶
本子	☆	🌶	🌶
足球	☆	🌶	🌶

Sentences			
这是谁的本子？	☆	🌶	🌶
那是不是你的铅笔？	☆	🌶	🌶
那是/不是我的铅笔。	☆	🌶	🌶

Ask who or whom someone is	☆
Ask and respond to questions about personal belongings	☆

3 What does your teacher say?

My teacher says ...

分享 Sharing

Words I remember

是	shì	to be
谁	shéi	who, whom
这	zhè	this
那	nà	that
男孩	nán hái	boy
女孩	nǚ hái	girl
铅笔	qiān bǐ	pencil
本子	běn zi	notebook
足球	zú qiú	football

Other words

献	xiàn	to dedicate
爱心	ài xīn	love
我们	wǒ men	we, us
他们	tā men	they, them
东西	dōng xi	thing
帮助	bāng zhù	to help
他人	tā rén	other people
吗	ma	(question word)

OXFORD
UNIVERSITY PRESS

Oxford University Press is a department of the University of Oxford.
It furthers the University's objective of excellence in research, scholarship,
and education by publishing worldwide. Oxford is a registered trade mark of
Oxford University Press in the UK and in certain other countries

Published in Hong Kong by
Oxford University Press (China) Limited
39th Floor, One Kowloon, 1 Wang Yuen Street, Kowloon Bay,
Hong Kong

© Oxford University Press (China) Limited 2017

The moral rights of the author have been asserted

First Edition published in 2017

All rights reserved. No part of this publication may be reproduced, stored in a
retrieval system, or transmitted, in any form or by any means, without the prior
permission in writing of Oxford University Press (China) Limited, or as expressly
permitted by law, by licence, or under terms agreed with the appropriate
reprographics rights organization. Enquiries concerning reproduction outside
the scope of the above should be sent to the Rights Department, Oxford
University Press (China) Limited, at the address above

You must not circulate this work in any other form
and you must impose this same condition on any acquirer

Illustrated by Anne Lee and Wildman

Photographs for reproduction permitted by Dreamstime.com

China National Publications Import & Export (Group) Corporation is an authorized distributor of
Oxford Elementary Chinese.

Please contact content@cnpiec.com.cn or 86-10-65856782

ISBN: 978-0-19-082144-9

10 9 8 7 6 5 4 3 2